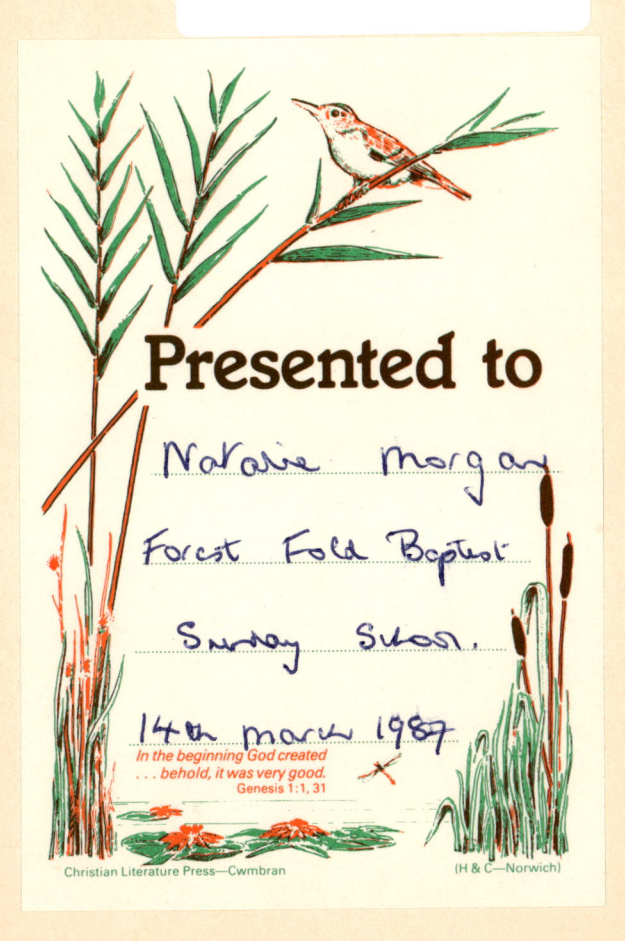

THE DOCT... UP

Presented to

Natalie Morgan

Forest Fold Baptist

Sunday School.

14th March 1987

*In the beginning God created
... behold, it was very good.*
Genesis 1:1, 31

Christian Literature Press—Cwmbran   (H & C—Norwich)

THE DOCTOR WHO NEVER GAVE UP

The Story of Ida Scudder in India

by
CAROLYN SCOTT

LUTTERWORTH PRESS
GUILDFORD, SURREY

First paperback edition 1975
Second impression 1984

ISBN 0 7188 2244 7

Copyright © 1970 Carolyn Scott

All rights reserved. No part of this publication may be reproduced, stored in a retrieval system, or transmitted, in any form or by any means, electronic, mechanical, photocopying, recording, or otherwise, without the prior permission of Lutterworth Press, Luke House, Farnham Road, Guildford, Surrey.

PRINTED PHOTOLITHO IN GREAT BRITAIN
BY EBENEZER BAYLIS AND SON, LTD.
THE TRINITY PRESS, WORCESTER, AND LONDON

CONTENTS

		Page
1	"Pasi" Means Hungry	9
2	"I Can Do Nothing"	16
3	"Pay The Sum of..."	26
4	Another Chance	35
5	"A Girl is no Good"	45
6	The Beat of Tom-Toms	52
7	The Devil Wagon	59
8	"But They're Only Women"	69
9	"It's a Miracle"	80
10	Anything is Possible	89

ACKNOWLEDGMENTS

The author is indebted for a great deal of her information to the following books:

Dr. Ida by Dorothy Clarke Wilson (Hodder & Stoughton)

Dr. Ida by Sheila Smith (Eagle Books, Edinburgh House Press)

1

"PASI" MEANS HUNGRY

IDA was cross because she was hungry. It was as hot as it can be in India, the sun beating down on the veranda. And now, when she wanted a second helping, her father said, "No."

"I'm *hungry*, Daddy!" she insisted. "Why can't I have some more? There's always more."

"Not today, darling," said Mrs. John, Ida's mother, cheerfully. She didn't look as cheerful as she sounded, but Ida didn't notice.

"I shan't do my lessons properly," threatened Ida obstinately. "I shall get ill. I might even..." she hesitated, searching for a fate dreadful enough, "I might even *die*!"

"Not a chance!" Lew, one of Ida's five brothers, got up in disgust and went out.

Dr. John, Ida's father, was a tall man. He had an enormous black bristling beard and deep, dark eyes. When he was angry, his eyes flashed and the red lights in his beard seemed like flames. For a moment, Ida thought he was going to be angry now. But when he spoke, his voice was very quiet.

He held out his hand. "Come along, child. We've work to do this morning. When we've

THE DOCTOR WHO NEVER GAVE UP

finished," he added, "when we've finished, there might be a second helping for you."

Ida had to run to keep up with him. Her starched linen dress was hot in the sun. She wondered whatever work she could do for her father. On Sundays, he preached, but it wasn't Sunday, and she couldn't give a sermon. Not at seven years old. Not ever, if she could help it. During the week he went round the villages, visiting and caring for people who were ill. Ida giggled as she thought of the little boy who came to the mission house yesterday with a pebble stuck firmly in his ear. She couldn't have done anything for him. She'd be no use there.

But there was one thing she didn't know about. Every morning her father had been out in the school yard at the back. She had seen him go there, and she had seen queues of children with their parents. Then it had been time for lessons and she had never known any more. Except that whenever Dr. John came home he seemed to look sad and his voice was quiet.

In the kitchen, bread was being broken up into a huge wicker basket. Her eyes widened. Second helpings and more and more of them. She opened her mouth to say, "I told you so," but, before she drew a breath, Dr. John had put the basket into her hands and they were off again.

When Dr. John opened the door on to the back yard, Ida saw the children.

"PASI" MEANS HUNGRY

There were hundreds of them, sitting in rows on the ground. Some had a few rags clutched round them. They were all sitting, waiting.

"Pasi, pasi," brown, bony fingers caught at the edge of Ida's dress. She looked down. A little boy without a stitch on was gazing up at her pleadingly. "Pasi," he insisted, tugging again at her dress.

"What does it mean, Daddy?" asked Ida. "What do they want?"

"Pasi means hungry," said Dr. John gravely, looking down at her. "They have nothing to eat. And that basket is full of bread."

Ida spent all morning giving out bread. The world seemed full of hands, small brown hands, clutching, grabbing, pulling impatiently, urgently. Hands that were sometimes so weak that Ida had to put the bread straight into an open mouth. And the only word she could hear was "pasi, pasi, pasi".

Bright copper bangles chinked on bony wrists. Ida looked down at a little girl and, as she pushed bread into her hand, she thought, "She's my age, she must be." Then she went on to the next, backwards and forwards along the rows. Soon she would have to begin breaking the pieces of bread in half or there would not be enough to go round.

There wasn't enough. Dr. John said there never was. And the children who had none could come first tomorrow morning.

"Why?" Ida didn't dare to ask the question, but

THE DOCTOR WHO NEVER GAVE UP

it hammered at her mind all the way back to the mission house. Why was there no food? Why was everyone hungry? Why were there children so weak that they couldn't have eaten for days? Couldn't have eaten for days—she felt the colour flushing up in her cheeks. She didn't dare to look up at her father.

But he wasn't angry. And he knew the questions even though she didn't ask them. And when they reached home, he swung her on to his knee and turned her face towards him.

"Do you still have to have that second helping, Idee?" he asked her solemnly.

Ida shook her head. Of course she was hungry—she always was. Her tummy was rattling around like the dry seeds in the golden pods of the Beggarman's tree when they swung to and fro in the breeze. But she didn't seem to notice it any more. "No, Daddy. No."

"In India, Ida, when there is no rain, there is no food." Dr. John pointed to the brown hills in the distance. They rose from the dull grey swamps of the paddy fields and climbed into the sky. To Ida, they looked as high as mountains. "Haven't you noticed how brown the hills are? How the brown goats can hide in them and you don't know where they are? And the fields all dry and grey where the rice hasn't grown, and the trees twisting and crumbling because they're so hot and dry and there is no water for them to drink?"

"PASI" MEANS HUNGRY

Dr. John lifted her gently off his knee. "That's what happens when there's no rain, Ida. When there's no rain, there's no food. And there's been no rain for over two years now."

The next morning, Ida got out of bed and went straight to the window. She strained her eyes to see the hills. Last night she had asked God to make them green again. But they were still brown. When the rain came, she knew it would be like magic, with the trees turning green and brilliant oleander flowers splashing the hillside with crimson. But there was no rain yet.

It didn't rain for three years. They called it the Great Famine of 1877, and more than five million people died. Every day Ida took round the basket of bread and every day there were fewer children to feed. And there was never enough bread in the basket.

"Pasi, pasi, pasi." Pasi meant hungry and Ida knew she could never, never, forget it.

* * *

She did her best to forget it when she was at school in America, and India was hundreds of miles away. But the pictures in the geography books were so pale.

"That's not India," Ida insisted one day when her teacher showed them a picture. Her India was vivid and exciting and noisy, not insipid and boring like a geography lesson. There were brilliant domes studded with jewels. There was hot red dust that blew into her eyes and spotted her dress. Chanted spells and magic in the bite of a cobra, brilliant birds that shrieked and piped shrilly all day long. There were months and years waiting for the rain. Try as she might, she could never forget it.

Ida liked school. She was popular and she enjoyed herself. She was good at games and she was always a ringleader whenever mischief was planned. Her long fair hair and blue eyes were always at the centre of trouble.

"And to think that child is going to be a missionary," clucked her teachers disapprovingly. And the older she grew, the more disapprovingly they clucked.

"I am *never* going to be a missionary."

"But your name is Ida Scudder," pointed out her American school friends patiently. "Of course, you'll be a missionary. You wait and see."

Ida thought of the red dust and the way the heat had made her clothes feel. She looked down at her long pale blue dress and dainty shoes. She patted her hair, piled up in golden fair curls on top of her head. She was nineteen years old. She was doing well at college. There was plenty of mischief to get up to, and there were boys to take her to parties and dances. Good-looking boys with sleek hair who knew nothing at all about India. Annie Hancock, her best friend, envied her. She longed to be a missionary but she couldn't see how she would

"PASI" MEANS HUNGRY

ever have the chance. She was shy, and she didn't say much, but Ida knew. And because she knew, she tried not to think about it. For some reason it made her feel uncomfortable.

"*All* the Scudders are missionaries," they persisted. Ida knew that. That was why her mother and father were miles away in India. That was why she missed them, and missing them made her hate the mission station and everything she could remember about it. It made her hate India.

Ida always had to be different. She loved rebellion. She loved it when all the odds were piled up against her. All Scudders were missionaries. In that case whatever she did, she was not going to be one of them.

"I'll *never* be a missionary!" she shouted angrily. "Never, never, never, never!"

2

"I CAN DO NOTHING"

"COME on, Idee!" They were going to watch the boys playing baseball up at the College. Everyone was ready except Ida. She was upstairs in her room staring at the telegram.

"Come immediately. Your mother ill and needs you." The words ran into each other and she read them again. "Come immediately".

"I don't want to." The immediate response welled up inside her. Defiance and indignation. To go back to India, to the poverty and the dust and the terrible, scorching heat. To leave America and all her friends. To leave the fun and the parties and the excitement of being nineteen years old. To leave it, even for a few months. No. She couldn't.

Your mother ill. Ida shut her eyes and remembered. She could remember her mother's eyes and the way they smiled even when they were meant to be cross with her. She remembered her mother stopping Lew from dunking chickens head-first in the water-butt by dunking him instead. She remembered the security of being hugged and kissed goodnight. Her mother was ill. Then Ida must go to her as quickly as possible.

"I CAN DO NOTHING"

"Come *on*, Idee! The game'll be over. Come *on*!"

Ida picked up her hat, rammed it on her head and ran down the street to cable back, "Coming first boat. Ida."

* * *

They lived in a house of sun-baked bricks, plastered with mud and painted with whitewash. There was a long, low veranda running the length of the three rooms and white ants clustered on the roof, scattering dust on the hard mud floor.

Ida took one look and thought it terrible.

"Darling, it's so wonderful to have someone to speak *English* to," sighed Mrs. John, hugging and kissing her a hundred times a day. "When Daddy's away, I talk to myself sometimes, I'm so lonely!" She looked thin and tired but her eyes still smiled. And although Ida had only been home for a couple of days, it seemed to her that her mother was looking better already.

Dr. John spent so much time away. As a doctor, he visited the homes in the village, and as a pastor, he preached in the local church. And it took him sixteen days to tour all the surrounding villages. Sometimes Ida went with him. She watched him baptizing babies, their brown bodies squirming and slippery with coconut oil.

"Where's Mrs. John?" asked the villagers in dismay when they saw only Ida and her father.

"What we call baby, Missee?" they asked. "Mrs. John, always she name baby." And they looked scornful at Ida's suggestions of David or John or Matthew, and insisted on Melchisedek instead.

Then they travelled on, and Ida watched her father preach for three hours on end in steaming hot mud churches. She heard him telling the story of Jesus from an outdoor pulpit while his voice was drowned by chanting from people dancing round the incense burning at the altar nearby. And she helped him tie up his long beard and watched him kneel down on a sheet to operate on people who had walked miles to come to him. People who went away marvelling at the white man's God who could make sick people well again.

One day as they were finishing the last operation, a man came running up to Dr. John.

"Doctor Ammal, come very quickly," he insisted as soon as he saw the doctor. "Not for me, it is for my wife," he explained, watching impatiently as the sheet was wound up and the last of the instruments packed into the bag. "Juldi, Ammal. Hurry, please." His eyes scolded and pleaded both at once. "She is very young," he added, and Ida felt sorry for her.

Dr. John's face was grim as they set off. Ida wondered why. It was getting late, but he didn't usually mind that. As they reached sight of the high stone walls, the short, sharp dusk was just

"I CAN DO NOTHING"

turning into night and the hills in the distance turning suddenly from blue to black.

"Which way?"

"This way, Ammal. This way." They hurried on.

At last they were there. To Ida's surprise they stopped outside the open entrance-way to the house, and Dr. John put down his bag and stood waiting while the man went in.

"Go on, Daddy!" Ida was by now as concerned about the girl as her husband was. She was impatient. When someone was ill, time mattered. "Daddy. Go *on*!"

As he started to turn to her a muffled call came from a dark hole in the wall some way along from where they were standing. Dr. John went towards it and Ida followed, for the moment her curiosity silencing her. Dr. John bent down to the hole and Ida craned round his shoulder to see what he was doing. Then she gasped in amazement.

A slim brown wrist was stuck through the hole in the wall and Dr. John was taking the pulse. Quietly, as he stood there, he asked questions. Was there pain? Where was it? How long had this been? What food, what drink, what sleep?

Even in the silence, the muffled replies were barely audible. The voice was shy. The words were whispered. Then the conversation was ended —and so was the examination.

"She should have treatment," advised Dr. John. The husband shook his head. "No, no,

THE DOCTOR WHO NEVER GAVE UP

doctor. The women will see to that. You give the medicine and they will see she is well. You are kind, doctor Ammal, too kind. Most kind."

Dr. John gave him a note to take to the dispensary in the morning. Then they walked back in silence. Silence, until the old question forced its way out of Ida's lips.

"Why? Why can't you go in? How can you treat anyone like that? Why? Why?"

Dr. John sighed. "It is the custom."

"But what's custom when a girl is sick?"

In India, girls married young. Many of them were thirteen or fourteen. Ida knew that the brown wrist belonged to a girl round about her own age, maybe younger. A girl who had probably never seen the hills or paddy fields or the scarlet flowers after the rain.

"It is their religion, Idee. We believe in right and wrong in our religion and to them, this is their right and wrong. They are Hindus or Moslems, very strict religious people. Their laws tell them that their wives must be kept hidden where no other man may set eyes on them. They have another law too, called the 'caste' law. That tells them they must only associate with members of their own caste—people with similar backgrounds, similar professions or trades, similar breeding. They never go to each other's homes. They never eat food together. The sweepers and the washers are called the untouchables and they

"I CAN DO NOTHING"

belong to no caste at all. But they believe that all this is right, Idee. And so long as they believe that, what can I do? I can take their pulses and I can prescribe medicine for them. But I can't see that they take it.

"I have to leave that to the women. And the women believe that cool water is bad for a fever, and clean water is unholy, and illness is the will of the gods to punish evil. They have never heard of gods who love, Ida. They've never heard of gods like that."

"But you tell them, Father."

"Yes. I tell them. And perhaps one day they will understand. But they don't yet."

Ida went to her room thinking about a girl who had no medicine but the camphor oil and the black tar from the woodbark, and no gods but the golden idols in the temple. And right and wrong seemed a very hard thing to understand.

"Perhaps one day, I shall understand." Unconsciously she echoed her father's words. "Perhaps one day. But I don't yet."

That night she sat up late writing a letter to Annie back home in America—Annie who envied her so much. Lizards darted up the wall. Ants chased each other busily across the ceiling. The oil lamp spluttered and flickered light across the room. Ida sighed. How she longed to be back home in America with Annie. Footsteps scuffed along the veranda and stopped outside her door.

THE DOCTOR WHO NEVER GAVE UP

People were always coming, day and night, to see her father. She took the lamp and went to see who it was.

It was a Brahmin, one of the Hindu priests. Ida could see his spotless white turban and the gold braid edging his long white robe. As he raised his hands in greeting she turned to take him to her father. But he had not come to see Dr. John.

"Please come," he begged Ida, his eyes pleading with her. "My wife—she is so young, and the baby will not come. They can do no more for her and she will die. Please come to her."

"My father is the doctor," corrected Ida gently. "I can't do anything for you—but he can. We'll go and ask him."

The young man stepped back from her, anger and indignation flashing in his eyes. "Another man in my home, caring for my wife? Allow another man to set eyes on her? She would be better dead."

For a moment Ida couldn't find words. She couldn't believe what she was hearing. She knew India. She knew now about the laws. But what were laws compared with life and death?

"I'll come too," she pleaded. "I'll help him. He will make her well. You must listen—don't you want her to live? My father *must* come. I can do nothing on my own."

"Nothing?" the young man questioned pleadingly.

"I CAN DO NOTHING"

"Nothing."

He turned away. He walked down from the veranda, his face grim and set, but his eyes sad. Then he was lost in the night.

The lizard still played up and down the wall, but Ida didn't see it. All she could see was the reproach in the young man's eyes because she would not come. All she could hear was her own words: "I can do nothing." She went back to her desk but she was too disturbed to write, wishing that she could have done something. Anything.

When she heard footsteps again, she leaped up so quickly she nearly knocked the lamp over. He had come back. It must be the Brahmin, and he couldn't let her die. She ran out on to the veranda.

It was a Mohammedan, one of the Moslems, with his white hat and black buttons shining all the way down his long white tunic.

"Please, Amma, you will come," he said, his hands clasped together, the words tumbling out. "My wife is dying, juldi, hurry, hurry. It is important to come quickly." He turned as if certain that Ida would follow, but she shrank back in the doorway. This was no second chance—it was a nightmare. "I can do nothing." Words that Ida was not used to speaking, and she hated them. "But my father...."

This time Dr. John came from his study and they reasoned with the Mohammedan. Ida would come too. There would be no offence. If they

23

didn't come, his wife would die, and didn't that mean anything?

It did—but the law meant more.

"No man outside my family will ever look on the face of my wife," he repeated emphatically again and again. "She had better die than that." And the scorn in his voice tore at Ida's heart.

"Why?" she begged her father, as they watched the man turn away, as the Brahmin had turned, away into the darkness. "Why?"

"You know why. It's their law. It is their right and wrong. We must respect them for it."

"*Respect!*" Anger choked in Ida's voice. "Respect?"

"Yes." Her father's voice was quiet and firm, but Ida knew that his heart was as heavy as hers as he turned and went back to his study.

When the third visitor came, the footsteps on the veranda and the timid knocking at the door. Ida ran to open it. Surely this time God was giving them another chance. But it was a high caste Hindu who begged her to come as the others had begged her. His wife was dying. Just a child, but in such pain . . . she could hardly bear to listen. The nightmare hadn't ended, although she was wide awake. And as he turned away in the darkness, she found herself compelled to watch until every sight of him had gone.

Ida couldn't sleep that night. A thousand miles away America waited. The opportunities, the

"I CAN DO NOTHING"

gaiety, the chances. Here in India, the India she hated so much, three girls within walking distance of her home were dying because she could do nothing to help them.

Ida prayed as she had never prayed before. Towards early morning, as dawn was beginning to come up over the hills, she went to bed. Before she lay down, she wrote in her diary: "I think this is the first time I ever met God face to face."

* * *

The sound of tom-toms woke her. The rhythmic beating that was a sign of death. Ida sent a servant out to ask and he came running back to tell her three women had died. "All three?" It seemed too hard to believe and yet she knew it must be true. And again, that strange compulsion kept her at the window while the drums grew louder and the women passed, wailing and beating their breasts, as the funeral procession wound its slow, tuneless way towards the spiral of smoke in the distance.

All three had died. And she had been unable to do anything to save them.

That morning, Ida knocked on the door of her father's study.

"I'm going back to America," she told him. "And when I come back here, I shall be coming back as *Doctor* Ida Scudder."

3

"PAY THE SUM OF..."

THE letter had come all the way from India. Ida held it in her hands, and looked at it, and just looking at it gave her a shiver of excitement. It was from her mother. Written on the front of it in finely formed copperplate letters were the words:

"Dr. Ida S. Scudder"

"We knew you'd pass, darling... but the joy!" All the news. India was still there, waiting and longing to have her back. The mission house at Vellore, the robbers and the rains and the inconveniences. And could Ida bring back with her a carriage strong enough for a man to ride on, and...

The words were just words. She would read them later. Ida put the letter back in the envelope. And she looked at it again, lying there in her hands:

"Dr. Ida S. Scudder"

* * *

Ida's fingers drummed impatiently on the win-

"PAY THE SUM OF..."

dow sill. Outside, the lilacs were in full bloom and the parks full of fresh green leaves. She stared at them and wished that they were the red of oleanders or the harsh yellow of tamarinds. Even the young green trees were not as beautiful as the stunted, twisted brown roots that clung to the brown hills in India. Red tape! Papers to sign and forms to fill up. It was all delay. And anything that delayed the sight of the great white boat waiting at the quayside to take her back to start work, was a nuisance.

"Dr. Cobb will see you now, Dr. Scudder."

Ida sighed. She had already seen Dr. Cobb, the secretary of the missionary board which was sponsoring her work in Vellore. She had answered all the questions and filled in all the forms. She had even persuaded them to put up enough money to send Annie Hancock back with her to fulfil her dream of becoming a missionary. What else could possibly be needed?

"I thought," she began full tilt, determined to get somewhere at last. "I thought if I began arrangements to leave for India now..."

Dr. Cobb wasn't paying very much attention. Smiling as she talked, he swung a chair round to face his desk, and Ida sat down.

"We have had a letter," he began, holding it in front of him, and re-reading it as he spoke. "It's from Vellore. They think there should be a hospital for women there."

THE DOCTOR WHO NEVER GAVE UP

"Oh!" Ida stopped dead in her tracks, thrilled with the thought. "Of course there should! What a wonderful idea." Already her mind was racing ahead, planning, imagining, seeing the joy on the faces of women who had known only the barbarity and torture of native remedies. Seeing the relief as they felt kind hands and saw kind eyes that cared for them. "It's what they've been waiting for."

"And we want you to raise the money for it," added Dr. Cobb, as an afterthought.

"Me!" Ida choked the word as joy changed to horror. "Me? Raise money for—for a hospital? But how much money?"

"Only eight thousand dollars. And you'll be lucky to get half that. Will you try?"

Would she try! Ida drifted out of the office on a cloud of amazement. It was like a dream—the most glorious daydream and the most terrifying nightmare all in one. To have a hospital for women at Vellore, and to be the one to make it possible. The most wonderful thing she could imagine. To have ahead the task of raising eight thousand dollars. Horror! The lilacs swayed in the breeze, but now, to Ida, they *were* oleanders. And the smell was the smell of musk and incense and rice cooking in the heat.

If Jesus said faith could move mountains, then Ida's tongue was capable of raising eight thousand dollars. She'd raise eighty if it was necessary. In the sunshine, nothing was impossible.

28

"PAY THE SUM OF..."

But spring turned to summer, and summer to autumn. And the sunshine turned into swirling mists that hung over the sea and made everyone feel damp and dismal.

"If you could *see* their homes," pleaded Ida to women's meetings and men's meetings, at conferences and conventions. "Imagine having nothing to heal a wound but boiling gum from the trees. Imagine having no cool water when you have a fever. Imagine having no hospital when you need one desperately."

"Terrible!" The women nodded to each other. It was a terrible state of affairs. But one had just bought a new house and another had just come back from holiday, and another thought perhaps it was all rather exaggerated.

"Can't you see it's life or death?" begged Ida, wearing her best hat and her best dress in the hopes of touching the heart of a millionaire.

But it was no good. The people who understood had only a few cents to give. And as November drew near, and the date of her sailing came closer, Ida had only collected promises of a few hundred dollars.

"A Scudder never gives up," she lectured herself in the mirror as she tied the bow at the neck of her tucked chiffon blouse, and adjusted her hat. She didn't dare think of the yawning gap between a few hundred and eight thousand.

"Eight thousand and not a cent less!" She told

THE DOCTOR WHO NEVER GAVE UP

herself, wagging her finger. "A Scudder never gives up."

Miss Taber was Ida's last hope. She lived just down the street with her brother-in-law, and she organized large meetings for women. It was a last chance, and it was a slender chance, but it was the only chance left, and Ida gave it all she'd got.

They sat and talked in the library. All the time they talked, Mr. Schell, Miss Taber's brother-in-law, sat in an adjoining room reading his newspaper. He was grey-haired, elderly and slightly forbidding. Ida tried to forget him as she talked. His presence disturbed her, but she was going to do her best in spite of him. He obviously wasn't interested.

She told about the three night visitors, and the words she still couldn't forget: "I could do nothing for them." She described the stifling courtyards, and treatment through a hole in the high stone walls. "And the rooms," she added. "When you are allowed in, they are so dark you can see nothing—and yet that's where you must operate. If there was a hospital for women, run by women, they would come. We could show them. And they wouldn't die when they're only thirteen or fourteen . . ."

Miss Taber smiled politely.

"Just imagine," ended Ida desperately in a burst of emotion, "if you had never seen the lilacs in the park. If you'd never seen the shops on Fifth

"PAY THE SUM OF..."

Avenue, or the great canyons, or the mountains reaching up into the sky. Imagine if all you had ever known was these four walls, without even a window to let in the light, all your life until you die!"

Miss Taber's face didn't seem to have changed. "You come and speak to my people on Monday, Dr. Scudder," she suggested politely. "Come by all means. We might perhaps be able to manage a hundred dollars or so..."

She showed Ida to the front door, and Mr. Schell lowered his newspaper for long enough to nod to her as she passed. Then the door closed behind her.

What was it her ayah used to say to her on the days when the rivers had run dry so that you could hardly see where they had been? Sometimes when Ida gently dislodged a pebble with her foot, and there underneath nestled a tiny drop of water, her ayah would laugh and laugh and say, "An ounce of water to quench an elephant's thirst, Miss Idee!" before scolding her for covering the toe of her white shoe with dust. A hundred dollars or so. Ida sighed as she climbed the stairs to her bedroom. But a few hundred would be better than none at all.

The next morning there was a letter waiting at the breakfast table. Ida poured her coffee before opening it. It had come by hand, not through the post, and she wondered who it could be from.

THE DOCTOR WHO NEVER GAVE UP

It was brief and to the point. Mr. Schell wanted to see her for a few minutes before the meeting on Monday.

"But Ida, he's rich!" exclaimed her friends excitedly.

"He has lots of money!"

"He might give you as much as—as a thousand dollars!" hazarded one optimistically.

"But he's cautious. It was his wife who gave money to charity, not him. And now she's dead. I wouldn't count on anything."

Ida wasn't. She was remembering the elderly figure sitting buried behind his newspaper in the corner of the sitting-room. She was surprised he had noticed her at all. Very surprised he had noticed her enough to write to her. She was intrigued. She was curious. But she was under no illusions. Mr. Schell was definitely not interested in hospitals anywhere, let alone in India.

When Ida was shown into the sitting-room, Mr. Schell was no longer sitting in an easy chair in the corner. He was sitting behind a desk, with a pad of paper in front of him, and a pencil in his hand. He had precise fingers, and his eyes looked right through Ida. She knew instinctively that no one could fool him.

"I couldn't help overhearing." He spoke briefly and abruptly. "I was interested. I would like to know more."

This time, Ida relied on her head rather than her

"PAY THE SUM OF..."

heart. Facts and figures, rather than emotions. She gave him percentages and population figures and statistics. She told him about building facilities and the price of labour, the climate, and even the soil composition.

"But qualifications," he muttered scornfully. "How can you, a medical student just out of college, run a hospital?"

Ida flushed. "I can't. Of course I can't. But my father is a skilled doctor with years of work in India behind him, and by the time the hospital is built, I shall have spent my year working as an intern under him. Between us, we will be quite capable." Their eyes met across the big desk. "If you have any doubts about my record at medical school, you are quite free to enquire there," she added.

"I already have," replied Mr. Schell, drawing his cheque book towards him. And suddenly his eyes met hers again, and Ida was astonished at the warmth in them.

"I want to make a contribution towards your hospital in memory of my beloved wife, Mary Taber Schell," he said, smiling as he wrote out the cheque in neat, precise figures. "You say eight thousand dollars, but I want this to be a really good hospital."

He tore out the cheque and pushed it across the desk. Ida stared at it in astonishment. When she tried to thank him, her throat was so dry she could hardly speak. But the cheque was there. It was real. She could feel it and she could read it.

"Pay the sum of..." and then the careful handwriting—"ten thousand dollars".

4

ANOTHER CHANCE

IT WAS eight o'clock in the morning. Ida threw up the shutter of the tiny dispensary and the sunshine streamed into the room. Rows of medicine bottles were ranged along the shelves. Bandages waited, neatly rolled, and, on the table, spread with a spotless white cloth, the instruments gleamed in carefully regimented rows.

At eight o'clock in the morning, the veranda outside the dispensary was still in the shade. On busy days, when Dr. John was at Vellore, queues of people would already have been clustering round the doorway waiting for their medicines and ointments and treatments. The noise of their chattering and gossip filled the morning air for a good hour before the shutters went up. But this morning there was silence.

Ida opened the window and looked outside. There was no one there.

And no one came the next day, or the next.

Ida had been back in India for five months. For four months she had worked with her father, gradually making herself known to the people, visiting the houses, treating patients, helping him

THE DOCTOR WHO NEVER GAVE UP

to operate. Then, suddenly, Dr. John had died. For days, Ida felt completely lost. She loved her father, and she missed him terribly. But she had also lost her teacher. Now, there was no one to ask for advice. No one to check a diagnosis. No one to ask for a second opinion. And now, when at last she had screwed up enough courage to carry on where he had left off, it seemed that no one wanted her.

To fill in the hours, she sat puzzling over Tamil, the most widely used Indian dialect, and Salomi, the cook's wife, flitted in and out of the dispensary, studying the bottles and jars, reading the labels, and asking questions. But still no one came, because Ida was a woman. She smoothed her long starched white dress, and ran her finger round the high boned collar. It was a stupid uniform for a country as hot as India.

Patience had never been one of Ida's strong virtues. She could stand it no longer. "Don't they know I'm here?" she demanded from the stable boy. And he shuffled uncomfortably from one foot to the other. "Didn't you tell them?"

He nodded. "They know, Missy." His eyes told her the rest.

"If only," she thought, "if only someone would come—anyone. But someone I know how to treat. Someone I can cure. Then they'd all come. If only they'd give me a chance."

The next day, as usual, she was arranging the

ANOTHER CHANCE

instruments on the table, checking and re-checking, though they hadn't been touched since she first laid them out, when there was a rattle of wheels and the crunch of pony's hoofs on the gravel.

The carriage was gaily painted, and the pony had marigolds plaited in its mane. The driver pulled up, jumped out, held aside the curtain veiling the carriage, and helped a woman out. The silk of her orange sari rustled as she walked, jewellery covered her arms. As she turned towards the bungalow, Ida could see that there was a bandage across her eyes.

Running down the path, slowing down as she reached the woman, Ida searched in her small Tamil vocabulary.

"Salaam, Ammal. I am the doctor. Let me help you inside." "And please, God," she added under her breath, "please let it be something I can cure. Something I can treat without operating. Please don't let her be blind."

As she took off the bandages and examined the woman's swollen eyes, Ida sighed with relief. It was a comparatively simple disease. She examined almost over-thoroughly, to be sure of making the right diagnosis. Then when she had done all she could, she called in Salomi to make sure that the woman understood the directions on the lotion she was making up for her.

"You must come tomorrow," she repeated to

THE DOCTOR WHO NEVER GAVE UP

her earnestly again and again. "You must come tomorrow and the next day and for many days after that. Otherwise you will go blind. You *must* come." And Salomi repeated it all over again, her brown face beaming with delight at the help she was giving.

The next morning, Ida was up out of bed and ready eagerly scanning the path, praying that the woman would come back. And she did come. And she came the next day. And on the third day, she brought another woman with her, and by the time her treatment was ended, Ida knew every morning as she went to open the shutters that there would be groups of men and women already waiting, queuing up and squatting on the veranda.

But that was in the sunshine of the Mission Station. And as Ida worked away, giving out medicines, soothing sores and taking stones out of ears and pebbles out of noses, there were still the dark shadows of the high stone walls and the tiny, dark shuttered rooms, steaming with heat and disease, which lurked forbiddingly in the back of her mind. The hole in the wall and the delicate wrist. The magic and the evil potions of the witch doctors and the village old wives, the superstition and the old women who had never seen beyond the high walls.

"Run and fetch Salomi," she called out of the window to one of the houseboys, as a baby with a fractured arm started to kick and scream. The

ANOTHER CHANCE

mother cowered in the corner of the dispensary, too frightened to help calm the child. Vainly Ida coaxed and patted and clucked, but the howling continued until Salomi arrived breathlessly, eagerness shining in her eyes, holding out her hands for the baby.

"See, Missy?" She stuck her hands under Ida's nose. They smelled strongly of soap. "All clean. You don't have to tell Salomi!" And slowly the howls subsided to hiccups and at last died away, while Ida set the bone as gently as she could.

Another success. Gratitude in place of fear, and the mother, whose screams had been louder than the baby's, was sent away beaming and laughing and full of joy.

Ida watched Salomi thoughtfully. She chatted and laughed with the patients, and gradually worried frowns and nervous fidgets gave way to smiles and gossip and pleasure.

"I wonder..." But there was no time for wondering. The patients came one after the other. By the afternoon, the temperature was 112° F. in the shade, and Ida was exhausted.

"The gentleman says it is most urgent," prompted Salomi a second time. "He is waiting outside."

Her petticoats sticking damply to her body, the white starched dress beginning to lose any freshness it had early in the morning, Ida stepped out on to the veranda.

THE DOCTOR WHO NEVER GAVE UP

"Doctor Ammal—it is my wife. So young, and the baby will soon be born. She is so ill. Please come to her."

Another chance! Even in the hot sun, Ida could imagine it was night time again. Then, there had been three chances. Each time she had failed. Now, at last, there was one more chance. And this time—how would she do?

"Take me quickly! Of course I'll come." She packed her instruments into the bag which she kept ready by the door, and together they set off for the town, the man leading in his fine carriage, Ida following as fast as the pony and trap would take her.

They arrived at last. Ida had forgotten the heat. Nothing mattered except success. The man was moneyed. He was a rich, high-class Hindu. He had education, he would understand and he would give her all the help he could.

"If only we're in time," she thought, praying that they would be.

They were in time.

They hurried through the inner courtyard towards the back of the house. Birth was unclean. It had to be kept in the dark. A little old lady, wrinkled and bent and brown as the brown berries, dried and shrivelled in the sun, beckoned to Ida. "This way, Ammal." Her teeth were stained with brown betel juice, and there was no smile on her face. Ida followed her into the tiny

ANOTHER CHANCE

back room, and the heat and the darkness seemed to smother her as she went in.

The girl was lying on a mat on the floor. The old woman stood as far from her as possible, and watched in silence as Ida bent over her and felt for her pulse. As she groped in the darkness, she called softly to the girl, but there was no reply.

"Is she dead?" There was still no reply. Ida's heart sank. She groped again for the wrist, and as she felt for the pulse, the girl drew her hand to her mouth and kissed it.

"Water!" Ida gasped in horror. The lips pressed on to her hand were dry and burning. The girl was dying of thirst.

"Water ... My medicine will not work without water!" Ida stumbled up and pleaded with the old woman. The shrewd eyes stared back at her blankly. The spirits forbade water. Superstition said that the sick were unclean. Evil spirits would lurk in the house and the gods would be angry, and ...

Ida kicked herself for her bad Tamil. If only she could have explained more. But the blank eyes forestalled any explanation.

"Please!" The heat was suffocating. "Please—bring me some water. Please understand!"

Slowly the old woman turned round and shuffled away. When she came back again, she held a tiny brass cup, with a few inches of water in the bottom.

"I need more water," Ida explained as patiently and politely as she could. "Much, much more water."

And she shuffled away and returned with a thimbleful more.

"I want all the water there is." But Ida knew there would be no more. The woman's eyes told her.

Brushing past her, out of the heat and the darkness and into the air of the courtyard, through the stone archway and into the outer courtyard, Ida went on until she came to the men, sitting talking and waiting.

"My wife! Ammal, how is she?" the Hindu sprang to his feet.

"She's dying," Ida told him bluntly, her mind seething with frustration and anger. "She's dying of thirst, because no one will give her a drink of water."

Tamil was forgotten. These were educated men. They understood English. "They are all afraid!" Her blue eyes flashed dangerously. "Are you afraid too? You men? Did education teach you to be afraid of superstition? To be afraid of spirits in snakes and sticks and stones? Or did it teach you to be afraid of your women?" She looked from the astonished circle straight into the worried eyes of the young husband. "What do you want? A dead superstition or a dead wife?"

For a moment, there was complete silence. Ida's

ANOTHER CHANCE

heart seemed to miss a beat, and her high collar clutched tightly at her throat. What had she done? What had she said? They might never accept her again, these men in the towns, the people she had come to India so desperately wanting to help. If only her tongue and her heart didn't run away with her so easily.

"What do you want us to do?" asked the man, almost in a whisper.

They brought the water. The women brought in pitchers of water, and Ida forced it gently between the girl's lips, and watched the flush gradually die down from her cheeks. And as the sun sank behind the hills and the coolness came, a baby boy was born—the greatest fortune the gods could bestow on a family.

When she arrived back at the Mission Station, Ida saw Salomi waiting for her, smiling from ear to ear.

"The little one with sore eyes was here again," she began eagerly, when Ida was hardly out of the carriage. "I told the mother to bring her back tomorrow. Shall I give her some of this?" She held up the solution of boric acid.

"Yes—but how did you know?"

"I have watched, Missy. I know."

"I wonder..." Now it was cooler. There was more time for having ideas.

"Salomi?"

"Yes, Missy."

THE DOCTOR WHO NEVER GAVE UP

"How would you like to leave working in the kitchen, and help me here instead?"

"Yes, please! Very much!" And Salomi clutched the bottle of boric acid and smiled with pride.

5

"A GIRL IS NO GOOD"

IDA could not believe it. At last the hospital was open. Forty white beds stood in rows in the two wards. In the operating theatre, a glass table gleamed, and kerosene stoves spluttered and puffed day and night ready to sterilize the brand-new instruments.

It was called the Mary Taber Schell Hospital after Mr. Schell's wife. Dr. Ida was in charge, and her only assistant was Salomi.

"Don't be afraid—she is our mother," whispered one patient to another.

"She won't hurt you," explained a little boy.

A girl shyly stroked Ida's white skin with her brown fingers, and a baby pulled strands of her golden hair and laughed in delight. They had never seen white skin and blue eyes and golden hair before.

"Come along now," admonished Ida as she came to an empty bed and a patient lying on the floor rolled in her sheet.

"But it is dangerous!" The black eyes gazed fearfully up at the high shelf that was apparently meant for lying on. "I shall fall off. No, I shall sleep on the floor!"

And a sturdy little boy recovered well enough from tuberculosis to attempt leaving the hospital one sunny day with his mattress on his head.

Ida worked from early in the morning until late at night. Sometimes she worked all night. Later, as more nurses came to the hospital, they were constantly at her door, their lamps glittering in the darkness, asking advice, asking her to come, and come quickly.

One night, she struggled for hours to save the life of a young Moslem girl and her baby. At last, the baby was born, a perfect, delicate little girl. But all the time, Ida could sense an uneasiness.

The relatives sat round. Often, with wealthy patients, almost the entire family camped at the hospital. They brought in food, and cooked it for the invalid. And they supervised every move. Piles of rice and beans were stacked away under the bed, and the girl's favourite jewellery glittered by her bedside. Silver and gold bangles, earrings and bright necklaces.

"It is a bad day."

Ida had expected that the birth would bring rejoicing. But the uneasiness continued. "The spirits are not pleased." The family sat around and shrugged their shoulders. "It is an evil day today." The grandmother clicked her tongue against her

"A GIRL IS NO GOOD"

teeth. "It is better no child was born today," and she shook her head.

"There," Ida decided the spell should be broken. "A lovely baby girl." For a moment she allowed them to look at the child, but none of them bothered.

"A girl? Pah! A girl is no good."

Tears welled up in the mother's eyes, and the family settled back glumly, eyeing the shrivelled little newborn baby, as Ida did all she could for her. Day and night for the next few days she watched over the delicate child anxiously until she was sure her life was out of danger. The shrivelled, newborn dampness gave way to big appealing eyes and strong little brown fingers, and Ida and the young mother cooed and clucked over the baby as if it was the first they had ever seen.

"Give them time!" thought Ida, watching the silent group of relatives out of the corner of her eye. "They'll come round. They can't help but love her," she thought, letting the little hands curl round her finger and patting the wisps of black hair.

"Isn't she lovely?" she smiled at them. "Isn't she healthy now? Soon you can take her home." But their eyes avoided hers as they sat silently, waiting until she left the ward.

Give them time. They would come round. They would love her. They must.

That morning, the dispensary was full. Queues of patients came forward. They seemed endless.

47

THE DOCTOR WHO NEVER GAVE UP

Outside on the veranda, sandalled feet and bare feet shuffled forward on the boards. Salomi fetched bottles and needles and bandages, rocked squealing babies, and comforted frightened mothers.

"There's something wrong with that baby!"

The voice in Ida's mind made itself heard quite clearly above everything that was going on.

"Don't be silly." She rubbed soothing oil on a sturdy brown leg. There couldn't be anything wrong. They'd tell her if there was. One of the girls would come from the hospital.

"Quickly! There's something wrong!" She had to listen. The voice compelled her to. Her common sense told her not to be stupid, but Ida had always been guided by impulse rather than common sense. If something was the matter, she must go.

Abruptly patting the child at her knees, she stopped massaging his leg, jumped up and hurried out of the dispensary, along the veranda, past the queues of surprised patients, giving them hardly a glance as she ran. And when she arrived at the ward, everything was so quiet that she felt rather silly, and nearly turned round and went back to the dispensary again.

The screen round the young mother's bed at the far end of the ward was in its usual place. Everything was orderly and quiet. You could hear a pin drop.

"A GIRL IS NO GOOD"

Something about the quietness roused Ida's suspicion. What was happening behind that screen? Picking up her skirts, she ran down the ward as fast as she could.

"No!" She pushed past one of the women and struggled to pull a pillow away from the other. "No! Stop it! Oh," she sobbed in rage and horror, "how could you?"

The pillow had been pressed tightly on the baby's face. Its cheeks were already blue. Ida bent over it, and at last it began to choke, and then to gasp, until eventually lusty cries were echoing the length of the ward.

She picked it up and rocked it gently in her arms. The mother was too upset with a mixture of relief and fear, to do anything but sob quietly. Ida rounded on the old grandmother and the other woman.

"How *could* you?" she repeated, trying to understand the sullen faces that stared back at her.

"It was the will of Allah." They shrugged their shoulders. "She was better dead."

"No!" Ida's cheeks were hot with indignation.

"You like her?" The old lady's eyes glinted craftily, "you like her? Then you take her."

Ida stared at her in amazement.

"You don't want her to die?" The old woman went on, taking advantage of the situation. "You can have her. That is good."

THE DOCTOR WHO NEVER GAVE UP

Ida looked from her to the girl lying in the bed. She had stopped sobbing. Their eyes met, and the girl's eyes were pleading.

"Very well." She looked round at them in cold anger. "Very well. I *will* take her!" And wrapping up her bundle firmly she stalked out of the ward and across to the bungalow, where her mother was cooking the lunch.

"There you are. She's ours." Ida deposited the bundle in a chair, and the baby began to cry again, even louder than before. "What are we going to do with her?"

"Feed her and give her a name, I should think," said Mrs. John, putting down her ladle and dandling the baby on her knee.

"Her family doesn't want her, and her mother can't have her . . . really, the hospital is her mother. So," she chucked the baby under the chin with the ladle, "so we'll call her Mary Taber."

* * *

And later, years later, whenever Dr. Ida had been away from Vellore, her return was heralded by feet running across the dusty courtyard, and children's voices shouting "It's Doctor Mother! It's Doctor Mother!" and a horde of wriggling brown bodies would rush up and throw themselves at Ida, hugging her and kissing her and clutching her arms and her hands and her legs and any bit of her that was within reach.

"A GIRL IS NO GOOD"

Because Mary Taber was only the first orphan that Dr. Ida made a home for at Vellore.

Padmathi, bright eyes peering over the mango she was sucking, had been found by a cowherd, crying in a thorn bush a few hours after she had been born. Ganesha had been brought to the hospital from the gaol when her mother died. Garuda and Krishna, shrieking and giggling as the nurses gave them their bath, had been found lying in the roadside, two little bundles of skin and bone. And Mana's mother had handed her baby to Ida the day before she died in the hospital.

"Please," she had whispered. "I know you will care for her. Because you love us."

And Ida did care for them. She loved them all. She carried them around on her hip like the Indian mothers carried their children, and when she went away travelling into the nearby villages, she always brought them back baskets of mangoes and bunches of oleanders and bougainvilleas, and watched with delight as the girls fingered the red flowers and fastened them in their hair. And she never minded when the basket was empty, picking up children, sticky with mango juice, and setting them on her knee and telling them bedtime stories.

And she never minded either, when the children gazed in fascination at her halo of fair hair, and Mana, eyes big with curiosity, asked, "Is it real?" And then shyly, reaching out sticky fingers, "Mana touch?"

6

THE BEAT OF TOM-TOMS

IDA was out visiting. She threaded her way through the narrow alleyways until she came to the street she wanted. The maze of high walls made it hard to find the way, but by now, she would have known it blindfold. This time, though, she sensed that something was different. Something was wrong. She turned into the street, and the sight that greeted her was chaos.

Bullock carts blocked the entrance. Men and women ran in and out of their houses, throwing rolls of bed linen out of the windows on to the cobbles below. Children were clamouring round, piling pots and pans on to the wagons. One man tossed a final bundle on to the top of the cart, swung himself up into the front seat between the rough wooden shafts, and set off with his family as fast as he could, so that Ida had to flatten herself against the stone wall for fear of being trampled.

"Where are you going?" No one took any notice. "What's happening?" A man ran past her, a jumble of belongings slung over his shoulder.

"What is it? What's happened?"

He turned briefly to look at her. There was panic

THE BEAT OF TOM-TOMS

and a blind fear in his eyes. Then he ran on without a word. Ida pushed her way past the carts and the stamping animals. Taking no notice of anyone, she went into the first house she came to. It was empty. Compared with the rush and panic in the street outside, it was strangely silent and still. As her eyes grew accustomed to the gloom, she began to make out the shapes of the few pieces of furniture left in the rooms. Then she went on through the house, until she stopped in the inner courtyard. There was a dark shape on the stone step leading to the back of the house. Ida went nearer to see what it was. Then, suddenly, she knew what had happened.

The dark shape lying on the step was a dead rat. It had died from a disease called the Black Death. Plague had come to Vellore.

When Ida returned to the hospital, it was almost empty. Families huddled in their homes and refused to let her come near to treat the dying.

"We must inoculate," announced the local Indian Municipal Chairman, his black eyes alive with anxiety and enthusiasm. "We must inoculate everyone. We must do all we can, and we must do it at once!" But it wasn't easy. Day after day, Ida and the ministry officials toured the streets, trying to persuade people to listen to them. But the plague was the will of the gods, and no silver needle was going to end it—nothing was going to end it but sacrifices in the temple, day and night, from the poorest as well as the rich. People as yet untouched by the disease took flight to the next village or to their home town miles away, and wherever they went, they carried the deadly plague with them. All night the fires blazed before the altars, dancing and leaping in the darkness as people brought gifts to please the goddess of disease. But disease spread with the rats, running through the streets, and leaving whole families dying in its wake.

"If only they'd listen!" exclaimed Ida in desperation, at the end of a long day. "We could stop it spreading. We could cure them." But wherever they went, fear was there first.

"If only we had a chance," the Municipal Chairman shook his head sadly.

One or two reluctantly agreed to allow Ida to inject them with the liquid in the long needle. But they were few. Most of the people she treated, she had found because their families had fled and left them behind, or because, from sheer persistence, she had forced her way into houses or pounced on children when she was quick enough to catch them in the streets. But at each house, she was greeted with blank denials.

"You have someone sick?" she asked the question again and again.

"No." The heads shook sadly. "None here." But their eyes did not meet hers.

"Why are you lying? Why can't I help you?"

THE BEAT OF TOM-TOMS

Ida was almost in tears, but their faces told her nothing.

"None here," again and again. "No. No one." Until in desperation, she could bear it no longer, and pushing past them with a muttered apology, she searched a house, through the outer rooms, on into the inner courtyard, and into the dark back room where incense burned day and night before the hideous carved image of the goddess of disease.

And last of all she opened a tiny back cupboard, and found a child, wrapped in rags, almost dead.

"Why?" she begged them, as she lifted the limp body out, "Why wouldn't you let me help him?"

"Because he is dying," said the man, his face closed and uncommunicative. "There is nothing you can do."

"Please, please, Ammal, leave here," begged an old woman kneeling at Ida's feet. "We hid him so that he can die at home, with us."

Ida went on with despair in her heart. Always it was too late. Back at the hospital, bottles of vaccine stood on the shelves, but fear made them useless.

"One day..." She knew it would come. But when? How long? Day after day, working alongside the health officers and the Chairman, she tried to do what she could, searching out the sick, persuading, arguing, cajoling, burning contaminated clothes, disinfecting homes, trying to

THE DOCTOR WHO NEVER GAVE UP

make up for time that was always irretrievably lost.

"Wait! Please wait!" A young man caught her arm as she was leaving an empty house. "Doctor Ammal, will you help us?"

Ida turned in astonishment.

"My little brother was brought to you, and you made him well. Now my daughter is sick." He hesitated. Then he took the chance. "Anything you can do, we will accept. I shall be most grateful if you would come."

Ida had no fear of the plague. She went with him as quickly as she could, and as soon as they reached the house, she treated the child as well as possible, and inoculated the rest of the family. Then they all came back to the hospital with Ida, while health officers burned the contaminated clothes and disinfected the house, tearing up the straw from the floor and setting light to it. A few days later, the young man brought a friend to be inoculated, and then the friend's brother, and his family.

But still the hospital was almost empty. Still fear preceded Ida wherever she went—a whisper and a scuffle of feet, a closed door and silence. Eyes watching, and turning away. Still the tom-toms beat continuously, as the death toll in Vellore rose to seventeen a day. But Ida was able to look at a healthy child, and know that a few people had been saved. And she knew that gradually, over the years

THE BEAT OF TOM-TOMS

of struggling and persevering, the vaccine would win. It would take time, but she had seen the proof.

"Very good!" The Chairman rubbed his hands. He and Ida had just returned from touring the streets together. "We're doing better. But we must have more—many more. How can we teach them?" he asked Ida, eyeing the bottles of vaccine still half full on the shelves.

"They'll learn—but not this time," she said gently.

He shrugged his shoulders. "Why not?"

"Because there is still fear. There is still suspicion. So many say yes, but then, when it comes to the point..." She knew that she needn't finish. If only, she thought to herself as she went wearily to bed, if only everyone was as enlightened as this man.

The days dragged on. Slowly Vellore changed from the happy sunshine town of scarlet flowers and cow bells jangling in the market, to a sad silence, broken only by wailing when the plague claimed another victim, by the throb of drums, and the grind of wheels and the clatter of ox's hoofs on the gravel as another family fled.

Three hundred people already dead. Ida and an Indian worker went to call on the Chairman to try to work out new plans. The plague had reached his street. There was the same panic. The same scuffling silence, and the same smell of fear. Even the atmosphere outside the house seemed strange to Ida—strange and unwelcoming. They strolled into the courtyard, and it was deserted.

Together, they searched the house, but it was empty. They called, but no one answered.

"They've gone!"

"But why?" Ida couldn't understand. "Where have they gone?"

"Back home—like the rest."

"But..." Ida was incredulous. "But they can't have gone. He was one of the first to insist that everyone was inoculated."

The Indian smiled at her ruefully and shook his head. "Yes everyone—everyone but his own family. He believed that Kali, Goddess of Death would be angry with him if he tried to cheat her. Nothing would have persuaded him to allow his own family to be inoculated."

Ida set her teeth and went on grimly down the street. There was work to be done. The sting of defeat always goaded her into action. She thought back to her childhood—to the children dying of hunger in the famine, and the brown hills, dry with dust in the drought, rising outside her bedroom window like high, dark mountains.

"What are mountains for," she asked herself again now, so many years later, "if they're not for climbing?"

7

THE DEVIL WAGON

THERE was a loud rumbling in the distance. A small group of people waited in the shade of the banyan tree. As the sound grew louder, they looked at each other in dismay. Some of them had bandaged hands and feet. Some shaded their eyes because they were so sore, and the heat of the sun hurt them. Some could not see because they were blind. But they heard the rumbling noise and a murmur of alarm spread through the crowd.

"What is it?"

"I'm going home!" one man started to elbow his way to the back of the crowd. "It's the devil, and I'm not waiting!"

There was a series of loud blasts, and a shrill whistle. And in the distance, a black shape appeared, jerking along at a great rate, entirely surrounded by a billowing cloud of red dust.

As it came nearer, the crowd scattered.

"The devil! The devil!" screamed one man, hobbling away as fast as he could.

"The devil!" echoed the women.

The noise grew louder, and the black shape grew larger as it came nearer.

THE DOCTOR WHO NEVER GAVE UP

"The devil! Get away quickly!" the children shrieked, flattening themselves behind the flowers, peering out from time to time, eyes round with fear.

Then with a series of explosive coughs and splutters, the little black car came to a shuddering standstill, and Dr. Ida stepped out.

"Where is everyone?" she exclaimed. And gradually heads popped out from behind tree trunks, and eyes appeared over the top of the flowers, until at last one daring child crept forward and poked out a finger and prodded the car. And when it didn't bite, and it didn't sting, he came a bit nearer and stroked the leather seat inside. Gaining more confidence every second, he prodded the round rubber horn that stuck out in front of the car, and nearly turned a somersault when it honked loudly in his ear.

But the spell was broken.

In ones and twos, sheepish, bewildered, questioning faces sidled a little closer as Ida opened the back of the car and put up a sliding table, laid a sheet out on it, and opened her bag of instruments. Meanwhile, Salomi, who had been travelling in the bumpy back seat, arranged bottles and jars of medicine.

The car was really a very peculiar sight. It was high and open. The wheels had huge wire spokes, and the little seats were hard and high. The steering wheel stuck straight up on a stick out of the floor, and when the clutch was out, the whole car

THE DEVIL WAGON

shook and shuddered so much that it was quite a task not to be thrown out. But as far as Ida was concerned, it served as a mobile hospital, and that was all that mattered.

The people drew nearer, and eyed her suspiciously. Haltingly, in rather bad Tamil, Ida tried to explain to them about medicine and treatment. But still they stood looking at her, no one willing to take the first step.

The little boy prodded the horn again, and nearly fell over in surprise at the noise that came out.

"Look." Ida went over, and bent down to him. He stared at her. Shy. Too frightened to speak, but too frightened to run away. His eyes were swollen and sore. He blinked back at her steadily.

"Look—do you like this?" Ida held out a gay picture card of flowers and coloured ribbons. The corners of his mouth twitched, and his hand came out. Then he drew it back behind him and shook his head shyly.

"You can have it. It's for you. And," went on Ida pressing home the advantage, "if you let me put some ointment in your eyes today, and tomorrow and the next day, they won't be sore any more."

His hand came out again. He took the picture, and smiled broadly up at her. Then he stood still while she let a drop of the soothing liquid trickle gently into each eye.

THE DOCTOR WHO NEVER GAVE UP

Just as she finished, Ida heard shouting. Bad as her understanding of Tamil was, she knew it wasn't friendly shouting. Turning round, she saw the headman of the village coming towards her, waving his arms in the air and shaking his fist. His face was brown and bony, and his eyes were angry. Patting the child on the head, Ida went back to the car and got in. It was no good. She knew she wouldn't be allowed to do anything more. The man stood watching her, words still pouring out of his mouth, and the people stood round and stared.

The little boy didn't care. He was gazing at his coloured picture. And as Ida was about to be driven away, a little girl touched her arm shyly.

"Please..." her eyes turned to the pile of coloured cards. "My brother is ill, and I couldn't carry him here because he is too heavy. Please give me a card for him." And in exchange, she held out a tiny bouquet of wild flowers, already beginning to wilt in the heat.

Instead of a card Ida gave her a doll in a coloured dress, and she stared at it in delight.

"Now I know he will get well, I know he will!" And hugging the doll tightly in her hands, she set off to walk the many miles back along the rough paths to her home.

It was a long way to Lathery, the next village. The arrival of the motor car at Vellore had meant that Ida could extend her work fifty and sixty miles

THE DEVIL WAGON

out from the hospital, and she made regular calls at appointed villages, starting early at six o'clock in the morning, and finishing long after dark at night. But always, when she tried to open a new "Roadside", as they came to be called, there was the same difficulty. People were frightened. The needles and the potions were less known to them than the bite of the cobra or the medicines of the temple goddesses. It took a long time.

Ida had already been stopping her car at Lathery every week for months. Each time the villagers looked at her disdainfully, and then turned their backs. If she approached a woman standing near a doorway, the door was shut in her face. The villagers were well-bred and very proud of their high caste. Ida was a stranger. Because she was a stranger, they considered her "unclean", and they certainly weren't going to accept medicines from unclean hands.

The cloud of red dust cleared as the car drew to a stop, and for the first time Ida found a crowd of men waiting for her.

"Ammal... doctor Ammal!" They came forward, and Ida heard the voices in delight. Getting out of the car, she turned to meet them and see what patient they had brought to her at last.

It was a bullock!

Ida looked at them in horror.

"Please? A cure? The Doctor Ammal will find a cure?"

THE DOCTOR WHO NEVER GAVE UP

To Ida's unpractised eyes, the bullock looked enormous. Its eyes were hot with fever.

"Please, please, doctor Ammal..." the owner pleaded. His bullock was his livelihood. The men stood round watching. Ida glanced at them. This was her chance to break through and establish confidence—if she could do it.

"Of course." She eyed the bullock firmly, hoping to mesmerize it into obedience. "Of course I'll do something." But what, she asked herself nervously, as the bullock snorted and kicked as she approached. The animal's eyes glowered at her, and they were anything but docile.

"Well," she demanded of the owner. "Can't you do something? I can't treat an animal while it's kicking me!"

After a struggle, the men held the bullock on the ground, and then they sat on it and kept it still while Ida examined it. Then she sterilized her instruments, and as quickly and carefully as she could, she removed a large tumour from the bullock's ear. Then they rattled off on their way again, leaving behind smiling faces and waving hands and demands for another visit soon, as the mournful wails of the recuperating bullock mingled with the honks and spits and bangs of the retreating car.

And as they rattled on, some miles away at the next village, a group of men were already waiting for the first sight and sound of them. They

THE DEVIL WAGON

were waiting apart, quite alone, on the outskirts of the main crowd.

"She will come," insisted a boy in a long white tunic. "Yes—but she won't come to us!" A man with twisted, useless fingers stared hopelessly into the distance. "No one will."

"*She* will." The boy knew what he was talking about. "She will prick you with silver that hurts like the bite of a snake, and then you will feel better." He touched his arm. "I know."

And his eyes had a brightness that the eyes of the others had not. They stood a little way away from the crowd, and no one spoke to them. One had no fingers at all. The other had both his feet bandaged. One had walked twenty miles from his home.

"You wait and see," the boy smiled, knowing he was right.

"Huh." Like most lepers, they had already given up hope.

Ida had come to this village before. Gradually, over the weeks, she had persevered, and now, at last, she knew that when the car puffed into the open space by the big tree, there would be a mass of people greeting her, holding up their bottles and jars for her to fill with medicines, letting her set broken bones and remove tumours and abscesses and put drops in sore eyes.

Over and over again, Salomi repeated the instructions. No, cotton wool was not to be eaten.

THE DOCTOR WHO NEVER GAVE UP

No, one swallow a day, not the whole bottle at once. No, the paper outside was not to be eaten, just the powder inside . . . And they listened carefully and went away, repeating the instructions over to themselves.

Now, they crowded round her, holding up their bottles. Mothers handing her their babies. Children coming up to stroke her hand or give her a little bunch of flowers.

Everyone knew that Dr. Ida loved flowers.

Last of all, when the crowd was nearly gone, Ida turned to the little group standing apart from the rest.

"You must be patient," she explained to them. "You will not be well all at once. You must come back again and again, week after week. The needle will hurt—but it will make you feel better." Eyes watched her doubtfully. "Now who's going to be first?" No one moved, and Ida's heart sank.

"Me, please!" A figure in a white tunic stepped forward eagerly.

"Abbai!" Thank goodness! Ida welcomed him with delight. He had come regularly, and the leprosy sores were slowly beginning to heal. His hands and feet were still numb, but she could feel his body quiver as she used all the strength she had to push in the needle with its large dose of healing oil.

"Ha! It's nothing!" he exclaimed bravely, determined not to show a twitch of pain to the

THE DEVIL WAGON

others watching. And after that, they all came forward, even the little four-year-old boy, who had gone without his breakfast in order to bring Ida a handful of rice as payment.

It was late when at last they started on the journey back to Vellore. The sky was dark, and the ruts in the bumpy tracks hardly showed, unless it was to cast fearful, grotesque shadows across the road. But as they neared the first village, Ida could see rows of tiny lamps flickering in the night. An enormous crowd of people were gathered under the banyan tree, and as the car came nearer, a man ran out into the road in front of them, waving his arms and calling at the top of his voice.

Ida recognized him. It was the headman. She recognized the bony face and the eyes. Her heart sank. What was going to happen? It was late and she was so tired. She felt she couldn't face trouble.

The car stopped. The headman came up to Ida and bowed and smiled.

"Good news." He smiled again. "The child, doctor Ammal. The eyes. They are much better." He pointed to rows of children lined up under the tree, watching. "If the kind doctor Ammal could treat all the other children with the same magic . . .?"

Ida was no longer tired. Even the rows on rows of children shyly waiting their turn didn't daunt her. Would she treat them? She treated everyone who came to her, setting up a lamp by the car and working as fast as she could.

"Your brother?" Ida recognized the large eyes turned up to her. "Did he like the doll?"

The little girl smiled, and pressed another bouquet into Ida's hands. "He has died, Ammal," she whispered. "But he held the doll close to his cheek, and he was so happy!"

And Ida went on, through the rows of little patients, then on to men and women brought by their friends in string cots slung like hammocks across their shoulders. Even the headman, who was quite well, brought along his bottle and asked her to fill it.

And when at last they were on their way back home again, Ida found that the car horn was missing.

"We must get another," she insisted. But the driver shrugged his shoulders.

"We make so much noise, everyone *knows* we're coming!" he told her, as the "devil wagon" spluttered and banged back to the hospital.

8

"BUT THEY'RE ONLY WOMEN"

A VISITOR gazed in admiration at a long white building, with stately white pillars and stone steps. As she gazed at it, a large cow walked out of the door and down the stairs and away into the gardens. No one took any notice.

"Did you say," spluttered the guest, "did you say that this is the—the new medical school?"

And, of course, it was.

* * *

Ida never did things in half measures. Every day, the queues of patients grew longer. Men walked miles to come to the red brick hospital to be healed by the white woman whose God made blind men see again and lame men walk. A second car was sent from America. Ida worked all day, and sometimes all night too. Often she arrived in the dining-room for breakfast at two o'clock in the afternoon.

"We need more doctors here," she announced one day.

"Will they send any more from America?"

"I don't know. But I'm not talking about

American doctors. I'm talking about Indian doctors."

"Indian *women* doctors" echoed her friends in astonishment. "But . . ."

"But what?" Ida swept aside their objections scornfully. "Women's brains are as good as men's and Indian women are as good as American women any day. And I'm going to prove it!"

Ida never waited around for opportunities to present themselves. She made opportunities, and then used them to the full. Not many months had gone by before she boarded the dusty wooden train to Madras, and presented herself before Colonel Bryson, the head of the British Medical Department.

"A medical *school*," she explained carefully. "We'll raise our standards to a college as soon as possible. All we're asking now is the chance to train Indian women for the Licensed Medical Practitioner diploma."

Colonel Bryson regarded her with amusement. "You've no buildings for students," he began, dismissing the whole ridiculous idea.

"We'll get them. Meanwhile, we can rent houses nearby."

"And you've hardly any money . . ."

"It's being raised. They are collecting in America. We'll get it."

". . . and no staff!"

Ida bristled. "I'm perfectly well equipped to

teach. One of my nurses will help me with anatomy, and the girls can learn physics and chemistry at the Mission college in Vellore. And next year, we'll be able to increase our staff."

"No buildings, no money, and no staff." He continued to smile at her patiently, although the smile was tinged with a reluctant suspicion of admiration. "We can't persuade Indian women to become nurses, let alone doctors, and if you do find a few who are willing, they'll be up against men, competing against them in examinations."

Ida got up in disgust. "You're talking about Indian women like an Indian man!" she shot at him as she made for the door.

"I tell you what..."

Ida turned and waited.

"You'll be lucky if you can find three girls who'll give it a try. But if you can find six—then go ahead."

Ida couldn't wait to get started. On the long train journey back, she drafted out a brochure for the printers. Before the first term opened in July, she had received sixty-nine applications, which she had weeded down to eighteen.

"Three if you're lucky!" she snorted. "If you can find six! What does he think women are? Cowards? Dunces? Layabouts?"

If he did, his suspicions might have been confirmed, had he attended one of the first lectures at the Vellore Medical School for women.

THE DOCTOR WHO NEVER GAVE UP

"What on earth possessed me to start a Medical School with a few books, a microscope and a skeleton?" sighed Ida, decking the skeleton with red ribbons for arteries, blue ribbons for veins, and yellow for nerves. Then she stitched muscles which flexed when strings were pulled, and covered the whole thing with a pale, skin-coloured cloth. One of the students fainted at the sight of it, and when Ida rang the local gaol for a corpse for dissection practice, three of the girls collapsed at the sight of blood.

"Please, please, let me go home," begged young Ebbie, Ida's favourite pupil, terrified out of her wits as the horrors of the human body unfolded themselves.

"Come along," answered Ida, comfortingly, "I'll take you with me to see a maternity case!"

Ebbie was terrified. Only Dr. Ida herself had kept her at the hospital for one second after she arrived. She was shy and nervous, but one day to be like Dr. Ida was a dream that outweighed all the gory nightmares.

But the maternity case was too much.

"Take me away! Please, please take me away," wrote Ebbie to her sister that night.

Next day, Ida took her to visit another patient. The patient was dying, and Ebbie was in tears.

"If you don't take me away, I shall leave!" she wrote again. "Or I'll die!" she added in desperation.

"BUT THEY'RE ONLY WOMEN"

Two days later, her sister appeared at Vellore, ready to take her home. She was angry, but there seemed to be no alternative.

"She's not going," said Ida. "I'm not letting her go." And the sister went all the way home again alone.

Several months later, Ebbie stood beside Dr. Ida in the operating theatre. Ida was about to operate on an abscess.

"Here you are, Ebbie," she turned to the girl. "Take the knife and make the incision."

Half in fear, and half in excitement, Ebbie took the knife.

"Don't be afraid. I'm right here."

The brown hands steadied and made the clean deep cut with perfect precision. Ebbie had got on top of her fears. She was notching up a regular ninety per cent marks each week in class. Ida watched her with satisfaction. She knew she had been right all along. Ebbie was going to make a first-rate doctor. And as for Ebbie, she was walking round the hospital with shining eyes, longing for the day when she, too, could do the things that her hero, Aunt Ida did, relieving pain and bringing smiles to sad faces, wherever she went.

"It's like watching Jesus at work," she marvelled to herself, watching the white-clothed figure move gently from bed to bed.

"If I have no love I am nothing" was the lesson

THE DOCTOR WHO NEVER GAVE UP

Ida liked to have read in chapel at the start of every week. "Love is patient, love is kind. There is nothing love cannot face. Love will never come to an end. Three things last forever; faith, hope and love. But the greatest of them all is love." And gradually the girls, as well as the patients, began to understand what the words meant.

But nothing ever happened fast enough for Ida. She wanted the end of the year, and the examinations—even if they brought failure. And however much she loved her girls, she was always one step ahead of them, and chastising them for being one step behind. One of her brightest pupils came running to her as soon as she summoned her from the other side of the building.

"What happened?" asked Ida, as the girl arrived. "Did you crawl?"

They went for picnics in the sunshine, and they went all together to parties in the town. But when they were working, they were working, and they were expected to work hard. As the end of the first year drew near, and the thought of the coming examinations loomed larger, tempers were strained to breaking point, and faces grew tense and worried.

Even Dr. Ida had her worries. "They'll be up against men," Colonel Bryson's words came back to her as she sat up at two o'clock in the morning, preparing the next day's lecture. "They'll have to compete against them in examinations..." And why not? Her girls were good. Ida was sure they were. But you could never be quite sure, and with so much prejudice against them . . . she buried her head in her notes, and tried to put examinations out of her mind.

The next morning, she arrived early in class.

"Good morning, girls!" she smiled round at them gaily. No one could have guessed that she had been up most of the night. "Now, this morning . . ."

"Please, Doctor Scudder . . ."

One of the girls stood up, hesitatingly.

"Please, it's a public holiday, and we wondered, we wondered," her voice faltered as Dr. Scudder's piercing blue eyes shot through her.

"We wondered if we could have the day off!" finished another girl.

"Holidays!" Ida slammed her book shut, her eyes flashing. "Holidays! Very well, you *can* take a holiday. Today and every other day too!" she finished, as she swept out of the room.

But when the girls went out and picked a huge bunch of oleanders and frangipane, all orange and scarlet and crimson and sweet smelling, Ida had to forgive them.

"We only wanted to catch up studying," they explained. "Please, Aunt Ida, please come back to us."

And because she was feeling a little bit ashamed of herself too, Ida welcomed them and carried on with her lecture, and laid on an enormous spread of tea and cakes in the afternoon, to celebrate the holiday.

"How will we ever pass?" the whisper echoed from one to the other. "What will they ask us?"

"How much will they expect us to know?" Books were hardly ever closed, and dismay greeted a bad mark at the weekly quizzes.

"We never learn much from success," comforted Ida, just in case they should turn out not to be as good as she thought they were. "Success makes you look up and the sun dazzles your eyes. Failure forces you to look down, and you mind your step. Those who can fail and learn, who can try and fall and get up and go on, who can make a new start and be defeated and still go on, they are the ones who succeed in the end."

Ebbie knew what she meant. But nobody knew it as well as Ida herself. Because each success had been built on failures. Every death she had seen had spoken of failure. Every time she looked into eyes that were incurably blind, every time she arrived at a bedside and found it was too late. But all that she had now, was built on that first failure, and the words that she would never forget: "I can do nothing." It was the failures and the setbacks, which, like the mountains, forced her to go on, to climb them, to beat them, to get on top of them somehow.

* * *

"BUT THEY'RE ONLY WOMEN"

"Dr. Scudder—good morning!" Colonel Bryson looked very bright and breezy. "I see you've brought your first class for their examinations."

"Yes. I've high hopes of them, too." Ida smiled at him confidently.

"You mustn't expect too much you know," he tried to warn her gently. "You mustn't be upset."

"Upset?" Ida raised her eyebrows.

"If they all fail," he explained.

"*All?*" Ida's heart sank for the hundredth time that day. "What do you mean, all?"

"Well, we can't expect too much, can we?" he comforted. "After all, you've only just started. And," he looked towards the group of frightened girls huddled together on one of the long hard seats put out for the examination students in the large entrance hall of the Medical School in Madras town, "And, they *are* all women," he ended, sympathetically.

Ida looked at them. Lizzie and Sophie, Thai, Anna, quiet, shy Ebbie, and all the rest. Fourteen of them had finished this first year with her, and were waiting to know how much they had learned.

"Good luck, darlings!" she called after them, as they were shepherded off to the examination rooms. "It'll all be all right. Wait and see!"

The examination lasted several days. Ida and the girls lived for the time in a mission bungalow nearby, and the atmosphere was tense and grim.

"That question about trachoma," began one of

THE DOCTOR WHO NEVER GAVE UP

the girls, but Ida wouldn't let them discuss it endlessly afterwards. One by one, the results from the seven men's colleges were posted on the board in the entrance.

"One in five!" howled the girls dismally.

"Twenty per cent—only twenty per cent passing!" They looked at each other in horror.

"We'll never get through!" And secretly, although she would never have admitted it to anyone, Ida was getting very, very nervous.

"If three of us get through," worked out one of them precisely, "I wonder which three it will be?"

"Not me!" came the unanimous chorus.

They were still staring at the meagre results when Dr. Ida emerged from the office of one of the senior Medical Officers. She had the pass list in her hand.

"It's all right!" They tried to read everything in her face. Her eyes sparkled with delight.

"But tell us—who's passed?" they clamoured.

"All of you!" Ida could hardly believe it either. Then they were all round her, trying to see the paper, unable to take it in until they had seen their own names, written down in black and white on that precious piece of paper.

"You've all passed," Ida kept echoing the words. "Every one of you!"

As she stood in the middle of the excited, laughing group of girls, she felt a touch on her shoulder.

"You've put our men to shame, Dr. Scudder!"

"BUT THEY'RE ONLY WOMEN"

Colonel Bryson shook his head sheepishly. "They'll have to work harder than they've ever worked before to equal a hundred per cent pass!"

"Don't expect too much of them," retorted Ida, on top of the world. "After all—they're only men!"

9

"IT'S A MIRACLE"

A BOY on a motor-cycle roared into the centre of the village. He pulled up in a cloud of dust, and went to find the headman. Ten minutes later, he rode away again, leaving only a cloud of dust behind him.

But that night, the tom-toms beat out a message, and a whisper of excitement ran through the village. Two days later, notices appeared on trees and houses in the main meeting places.

"Have you heard . . .?"

"Did you know . . . ?"

A boy pulled his grandfather towards one of the notices. "Grandfather, that's what it says," he insisted. "I tell you it *is*!"

"Don't believe it." The old man would go no further. The boy went nearer and read out loudly:

"Anyone with an eye disease—that's what it says, Grandfather. I told you. Come to the rice mill the day after tomorrow for an examination and, if necessary, an operation."

"Huh!" the old man spat on the ground. "And how much would that cost?"

"IT'S A MIRACLE"

"Nothing! It says that too—if the patient cannot afford to pay, treatment will be given free of charge! Honestly, Grandfather," the boy ran back to the old man, "give it a try. Just imagine."

The old man was imagining. But it was so long since he had been able to see clearly, that he had almost forgotten.

"It won't work." He shook his head sadly. "It never does. And this time won't be any different."

"But you will come."

"I—No—I don't know." He wasn't to be persuaded so easily.

But Krishna had other friends too. He had friends of his own age who were going blind. Abbai, who had scratched his eye with a straw, and little Gadanai, whose eyes were always inflamed and sore. He ran off to tell them the news.

"Come on!" They listened warily. "Give it a try!" He kept on and on at them. "I'll come with you. Just imagine."

But so many of them had never known what it was like to see properly, and it was hard to imagine.

Two days later, a blue van rumbled into the village. Behind it bumped a trailer, piled high with grass mats and pillows, food and dressings, lanterns and oil and medical supplies. The two senior doctors, their nurses and orderlies and the cook got out, and the headman escorted

THE DOCTOR WHO NEVER GAVE UP

them through the whitewashed houses, through the mud and thatch huts where the poor people lived, to the warehouse attached to the rice mill.

When they went inside, there were 300 people crushed together, waiting to be treated.

Tables were set up and instruments unpacked. Then, one by one, the patients came forward.

Krishna led his grandfather to the nearest doctor, and watched while he knelt down and let the man shine a torch first into one eye, then the other. All the time, he was muttering and grumbling.

"No good. Don't know why I came. Don't know what you're bothering for!" Krishna tried to shut him up, until he caught the doctor's eye, and the doctor smiled cheerfully.

"You wait a while," he said gently, writing something down on a tag and pinning it to the old man's ragged clothes. "Perhaps in a week or so, we'll know why I'm bothering." He turned to Krishna. "Take him to the nurse over there. She'll take care of him from now on."

Krishna obeyed, hardly knowing what he was doing. He had been staring at the man's hands while he worked. He had never seen a doctor working before. And had never seen anything so gentle. As soon as he could, he was back again, standing and watching, as patient after patient came forward to kneel down and let the

"IT'S A MIRACLE"

doctors examine their eyes. As the sun went down, lanterns were lit, and still the patients came. Eventually, way into the night, the last one went away.

"We'll start operating as soon as it's light tomorrow." One of the doctors turned to his nurse. "How many have we?" She looked towards the patients who had been kept in the impromptu warehouse ward for the night. They were lying on the grass mats, drinking gruel prepared for them by the cook and the orderlies. Each one had a tag sewn on to his clothing explaining exactly what operation was needed, and which eye was affected.

"There's seventy," she said.

They started early. Two long tables were set up, scrubbed clean and white. Each member of the team had a job to do, and for the whole of the day, twelve long, intense hours, they did that job with every ounce of skill and attention and energy they could muster. Krishna crept in unnoticed, and stood silently in the shadows, watching. Between them, the doctors could do an average of six operations in an hour. There was the intense silence of concentration broken only by occasional requests for instruments. As each operation was completed, the patient was made comfortable on one of the grass mats, arranged down both sides of the warehouse like a hospital ward, men one side, women the other. The shining silver

THE DOCTOR WHO NEVER GAVE UP

instruments chinked and clattered, and nurses patiently bandaged one head after another.

Krishna watched his grandfather, quieter now, led to one of the mats. He watched his friends. And he wondered. He had heard that the doctors believed in a God who could make miracles. But as he watched, these men seemed to be making miracles with their own hands. Late, late that night, he made his way home, and curled up on the earth floor of the hut where he lived. And when he went to sleep, he dreamed of a starched white coat, and it was his. And it was his hands holding the shining silver instruments.

The ride back in the blue van to Vellore was a long one. It was over in almost complete silence. Everyone was too tired to talk. Eye camps were a new occurrence, and they took every scrap of energy that was left after a long, busy week in hospital. The ten days ahead would mean fitting in the long journey five times, in between regular work, to change dressings and see how the patients were coming along. Meanwhile, four orderlies and the cook were left behind to care for them.

"Krishna, what's the hurry!" called his mother ten days later. She had never seen him up so early. "Where are you going?"

"It's today!" he shouted back over his shoulder, as he hurried off, leaving her none the wiser. Long before breakfast time, he was

"IT'S A MIRACLE"

out on the village boundaries, shading his eyes, searching in the distance for the first sight of the blue van, bringing the doctor back to the village.

He had watched them sewing up the wounds they had made, sewing them so carefully, with such fine stitches. Now they were coming back, and the stitches would be undone. Krishna could hardly wait. And yet, in spite of his excitement, all the time there was a sick dread in the back of his mind. How could anyone, even these new heroes of his, from the hospital at Vellore, make a blind man see again?

Then he saw them coming. And when he waved, they waved back to him.

"Here you are," as they climbed down, one of the doctors handed out a box of medicines to the little boy smiling up at him. "If you want to help, carry these."

If he wanted to help! Krishna marched proudly with them through the village, hugging his precious box of ointments to his chest. He was part of the Vellore Medical Mission!

That was the beginning of a morning Krishna never forgot.

Wearing gauze masks, the doctors began to work. While they worked, hot lamp sterilizers burned beside them, as nurses sterilized the instruments before handing them over. While an attendant held a torch, Krishna watched one

THE DOCTOR WHO NEVER GAVE UP

of the nurses apply drops of anaesthetic and then the doctor removed the stitches from his grandfather's eyes.

"You won't see immediately," they had warned. Now the warning was repeated. Bewildered by all that had happened, the old man blinked his wrinkled eyelids once or twice. Then he looked towards Krishna.

"What can you see?" The doctor was watching him carefully.

The old man hesitated. "Shapes. Dim, dark shapes," he whispered. "I couldn't see shapes before!" He pointed in Krishna's direction. "That's Krishna! I'd know his shape anywhere, the rascal. What's he doing here?" he asked indignantly.

"I'm not quite sure," the doctor smiled. "Can you see that lamp?" He kept asking questions. "Can you see this book? This bottle of medicine? These words?"

"No." Krishna's heart sank. "No. I think so —perhaps—no." What good were dark shapes in a land of light and brilliance and sunshine?

"Right. Now try these." The doctor held out a strange thing that Krishna had never seen before. Two round pieces of glass, joined together with metal. Curiosity got the better of disappointment, and he watched, fascinated.

A nurse took the pair of glasses and put them gently in front of the old man's eyes. And for the

"IT'S A MIRACLE"

first time in years, Krishna saw his face break into an enormous smile.

"Grandfather...?" But the old man wasn't listening. He was looking round about him. He was looking at the people. The doctors and the nurses, all dressed in white. At the sun trying to shine through the cracks in the corrugated roof. At the flames flickering and spluttering in the lamp. At the excited faces round him. The faces of Abbai and Gadanai, full of smiles and laughter.

"I can see!" he whispered. "I can see again! It's a miracle."

* * *

"It's a miracle!" Ida listened to the stories they brought back to her. She was eighty years old, and her white hair shone like a halo round her head. "It's a miracle." The original hospital had spread and spread. Students had graduated and gone out to every part of India, taking with them the knowledge and the love she had taught. And now, every day brought in new stories, new miracles, new discoveries, new cures.

She opened a letter addressed simply "Dr. Ida. India." It was a letter saying thank you. There was another one, addressed in the same way. It contained five shillings from an English girl's money box. She smiled, and strolled out of the door, down the wide white steps into the cool perfume of the garden.

THE DOCTOR WHO NEVER GAVE UP

"Please..." A shy voice stopped her. "Please..." Krishna's eyes gazed up into hers, full of trepidation. He had never seen a lady with white hair before. And blue eyes. He was struck dumb.

"Please, I want to be a doctor." The words tumbled out in a rush, and Ida laughed and took his hand, and walked him up and down the garden while they talked about it. Krishna could go to the mission school nearby. He must work hard, and learn a lot. He must say his lessons every day, and never think of giving up. And then—well, what on earth was there to prevent him being a doctor?

"Here?" Krishna was captivated by the sparkling blue eyes.

"Why not?"

Because that was one miracle that Ida had never in her wildest dreams imagined. Vellore was now a college for training men, as well as women.

10

ANYTHING IS POSSIBLE

"IT'S a miracle!" How often Dr. Ida breathed those words, as she grew older, and spent more and more time watching and marvelling while other people did the work. Modern science, modern medicine—wonders that she once dreamed of but never believed could really happen. Now she watched spellbound as a doctor examined his patient.

"Do what you want." The words were said bitterly. The young Hindu had leprosy. His hands were grotesque, like claws with the fingers misshapen and clenched tightly into his fists. "They're no good to me." No good for picking up rice. No good for anything but begging.

"I want to operate." The doctor was almost as young as his patient. He was from England. His name was Paul Brand.

"Do what you want," he repeated. "I don't care." And he shrugged his shoulders hopelessly.

Paul Brand did what he wanted. Day after day, he studied the muscles in the young man's arm. He moved the elbow and the shoulder. Then

THE DOCTOR WHO NEVER GAVE UP

he began to operate. And all the time, his patient answered without expression.

"No. No, I feel nothing. No—nothing. What's the use of it all, anyway?"

Ida watched the operations. Gradually the muscles from one arm were transferred to one of the patient's hands in the hope that they would be able to do the work the paralysed muscles could not do. There were several operations, each one difficult and intricate. As she watched the young doctor's face, Ida recognized the eagerness that she had felt, exploring, searching, finding out. But he looked so young. What could he do, this boy, she asked herself, against something like leprosy?

After the final operation, the patient's hand was encased in a plaster cast. The cast was heavy, but he accepted it, as he had accepted all the rest, in silence.

"What can you do?" Ida asked, in fascination.

"I don't know." The young doctor looked her straight in the eyes. "I just know what I should be able to do." He had longed for this chance since the first time he put out his hand to shake the hand of a leper. The boy was so stunned at the gesture that he moved his fingers and gripped the doctor's hand hard in return.

"There is something there," Paul insisted time and again after that. "If only I can find the way." Day after day, he had treated the leprosy patients

ANYTHING IS POSSIBLE

who came to him, some of them almost out of their minds, thrown out of their homes and cast aside by their family and friends. Others came with terribly diseased arms and legs because leprosy caused numbness, and when their flesh was numb, they didn't realize when a thorn stuck in a hand, or a cut turned septic.

"If only he can do it!" thought Ida to herself, in the tense silence, days later, as she watched the doctor slowly sawing through the layers of plaster to release the hand.

And now, even the patient was interested. His eyes were intent on the hands holding his. The cast fell off, and slowly the bandages were unwound.

What was Paul Brand thinking, Ida wondered, as she watched him, standing there, in her hospital, part of her own life, trying to do something that had never been attempted or even thought of before.

Gently, he touched the flesh between his hands. He rubbed the fingers and smoothed the skin, working the blood into circulation, stretching the fingers, moving them, testing them.

"All right." He looked up at the Hindu. "How about using it?"

The boy's face was impassive. He looked as if he hadn't heard the words. But slowly, he lifted the hand and looked at it. Then he lifted the other hand, a messy, twisted lump. They were

THE DOCTOR WHO NEVER GAVE UP

all looking at those two hands, side by side. His eyes went from the long, straight fingers, to the curled claw. And the room was quite silent.

As if afraid the fingers would break, he moved one slowly, and then another. Then he moved the thumb. Then he put out his hand towards the pieces of broken plaster lying on the table. Ida held her breath. But Paul Brand was watching with certainty on his face. Stiffly, but firmly, the boy picked up a piece of plaster and held it in his hand.

Looking across at the doctor he smiled. For the first time for years, happiness shone in his eyes.

"It isn't mine," he said quietly, lifting the new hand to his face and letting the smooth skin touch his cheek. "This hand you've given me—it belongs to your God."

* * *

New hands. New eyes. New life. Ida stood in her hospital and remembered the first days, in a tiny dispensary twelve feet by ten feet, when the patients wouldn't come. And now—it was impossible to see ahead. Anything could be done. On the wall beside her, there was a painting of Jesus. Behind Him, the artist had painted the brown hills of Vellore, rising into the blue sky, but Jesus seemed to tower above them.

Ida smiled. At last, she understood. The great

mountains in the distance were only really hills after all. But you didn't discover that until you had climbed them.

DR. IDA'S PRAYER

(taken from her diary)

Father, whose life is within me, and whose love is ever about me, grant that Thy life may be maintained in my life today and every day, as with gladness of heart, without haste or confusion of thought, I go about my daily tasks, conscious of ability to meet every rightful demand, seeing the larger meaning of little things, and finding beauty and love everywhere. In the sense of Thy presence, may I walk through the hours, breathing the atmosphere of love rather than anxious striving.